MW00811626

04-24

$3

The

A

to

Zen

of

Writing

Kathrin Lake

BUDDHA PRESS

in
association with
Vancouver School of Writing

Copyright © 2012 Kathrin Lake

All rights reserved. No part of this publication may be reproduced, stored in a retrieval system or transmitted in any form or by any means – electronic, mechanical, photocopying, and recording or otherwise – without the prior written permission of the author and publisher with exception of quotes from other authors. To perform any of the above, other than the exceptions, is an infringement of copyright.

For information on discounts for bulk purchases please contact director@vancouverschoolofwriting.com

To find other books by this author please go to www.kathrinlake.com

Printed in Canada

Library and Archives Canada Cataloguing in Publications
ISBN: 978-0-9881041-4-3

A to Zen

26 Reflections

26 Quotes

26 Project Pages
with Brainstorm Questions
for you to answer

There are no wrong answers.

Contents

_____

_____

_____

_____

_____

_____

_____

_____

_____

_____

_____

_____

_____

_____

_____

_____

_____

_____

_____

_____

_____

_____

_____

_____

_____

_____

A is for Authenticity

Authenticity is the process to find something that is
unique to you, whether it is a story, style, or what is
called voice. Even the most celebrated are not sure how
they acquired a voice except to
keep writing,
reading,
listening,
trying things,
borrowing,
begging,
stealing,
learning,
experiencing life
and seeing what sticks.

AUTHOR QUOTE

A is for **Acker,** Kathy

"I might be writing what people expect me to write, writing
from that place where I might be ruled by economic
considerations. To overcome that, I started working with my
dreams, because I'm not so censored when I use dream
material."
"I found my voice was a reaction to all that voice stuff... But
I still don't have a clear idea of what my voice is."

_____

_____

_____

_____

_____

_____

_____

_____

_____

_____

_____

_____

_____

_____

_____

_____

_____

_____

_____

_____

_____

_____

_____

_____

_____

_____

_____

_____

_____

_____

_____

_____

_____

_____

_____

_____

_____

Date: _____

Writing Project: _____

Q: What is Authentic about this project? And, how is that important?

_____
_____
_____
_____
_____
_____
_____
_____
_____
_____
_____
_____
_____
_____
_____
_____
_____
_____
_____
_____
_____

_____

_____

_____

_____

_____

_____

_____

_____

_____

_____

_____

_____

_____

_____

_____

_____

_____

_____

_____

_____

_____

_____

_____

_____

_____

B is for Being Bad

Are you shackled by the idea that you have to be good?

Anne Lamott taught us to accept that we all need to write
"shitty first drafts," but ask yourself another question:
Is trying to always "be good" good for our writing?

Why not try being bad and see where it takes you?
Where does it take your word choices?
Where does it take your thoughts?
Where does it take your stories?
Where does it take your characters?
(Are they being far too good too?)

Let go of being good. Bad is better. Liberate yourself.
See where bad takes you.
You can always go good later.

AUTHOR QUOTE
B is for **Bach,** Richard
"Bad things are not the worst things that can happen to us.
Nothing is the worst thing that can happen to us!"

_____

_____

_____

_____

_____

_____

_____

_____

_____

_____

_____

_____

_____

_____

_____

_____

_____

_____

_____

_____

_____

_____

_____

_____

_____

_____

Date: _____

Writing Project: _____

Q: How can Being Bad make this project even better?

_____

_____

_____

_____

_____

_____

_____

_____

_____

_____

_____

_____

_____

_____

_____

_____

_____

_____

_____

_____

_____

_____

_____

_____

_____

_____

_____

_____

_____

_____

_____

_____

_____

_____

_____

_____

_____

_____

_____

_____

_____

_____

_____

_____

_____

_____

_____

_____

C is for Character

The characters that live inside you,
The characters that you create,
The characters that you meet,
The characters that inspire you,
The strength of character that you possess to do what you do.
All are honorable.

There is nothing more satisfying, endearing or compelling to
know you have had the power to create a character that can
be deeply loved, hated, or some of both.
Imagine if there was no Scarlett O'Hara or Rhett Butler,
no Sherlock Holmes or Dr. Watson,
no brooding Hamlet, no Madame Bovary, no Hannibal Lecter,
no intrepid Harriet the Spy, and no Ebenezer Scrooge.
Life would be unthinkable.
Who is the next character? Can you give birth to one?
Explore character creation. Do some background work, listen,
watch, and ask questions. The detective work to find the keys
that unlock your character and your character's story is an
epic journey that you don't have to leave home to take.

AUTHOR QUOTE
C is for Christie, Agatha
"There is nothing more thrilling in this world,
than having a child that is yours, and yet is
mysteriously a stranger."
…"Every murderer is probably somebody's old friend."

_____

_____

_____

_____

_____

_____

_____

_____

_____

_____

_____

_____

_____

_____

_____

_____

_____

_____

_____

_____

_____

_____

_____

_____

Date: _____

Writing Project: _____

Character: _____

Q: What do you <u>not</u> know about your Character that you would like to know? Try asking your Character the question and write the answer as it comes.

_____
_____
_____
_____
_____
_____
_____
_____
_____
_____
_____
_____
_____
_____
_____
_____
_____
_____
_____

_____

_____

_____

_____

_____

_____

_____

_____

_____

_____

_____

_____

_____

_____

_____

_____

_____

_____

_____

_____

_____

_____

_____

_____

_____

D is for Discipline

Discipline is a scary word for many of us,
yet it derives from the same word for disciple,
someone who learns and then teaches.

When we write, we are both the teachers and the learners.
We are the chroniclers.
The pace at which we do this is up to us.
As long as we persist, is the only thing that will
ultimately matter to anyone.

AUTHOR QUOTE

D is for Dinesan, Isak

"When you have a great and difficult task, something perhaps
almost impossible, if you only work a little at a time, every
day a little, suddenly the work will finish itself.

Isak Dinesan was **Baroness Karen Von Blixen** of *Out of Africa* fame,
who wrote in an age when women habitually took men's names
and sometimes still do.

_____

_____

_____

_____

_____

_____

_____

_____

_____

_____

_____

_____

_____

_____

_____

_____

_____

_____

_____

_____

_____

_____

_____

_____

_____

_____

_____

Date: _____

Writing Project: _____

Q: How can I create a writing Discipline for this project
that is also a learning experience?

_____
_____
_____
_____
_____
_____
_____
_____
_____
_____
_____
_____
_____
_____
_____
_____
_____
_____
_____
_____
_____
_____

_____

_____

_____

_____

_____

_____

_____

_____

_____

_____

_____

_____

_____

_____

_____

_____

_____

_____

_____

_____

_____

_____

_____

_____

_____

E is for Enthusiasm

En Theos = God Within
When you have passion and enthusiasm for what you write
(or could be writing) it shines through.
Ask yourself where is my fire?
Where is my enthusiasm?
That is where you find your best work.
Composers, writers and artists used to say that they created
"by the grace of God,"
or by the God Within, En Theos.

AUTHOR QUOTE
E is for Eliot, George
"Adventure is not outside man; it is within.

Evans, Mary Anne (1819 –1880), better known by her pen name
George Eliot, was a leading English novelist of the Victorian era
known for her realism and psychological insight.

_____

_____

_____

_____

_____

_____

_____

_____

_____

_____

_____

_____

_____

_____

_____

_____

_____

_____

_____

_____

_____

_____

_____

_____

_____

_____

_____

_____

_____

_____

Date: _____

Writing Project: _____

Q: Where is my Enthusiasm for this project? How can I best capture that on the page?

_____
_____
_____
_____
_____
_____
_____
_____
_____
_____
_____
_____
_____
_____
_____
_____
_____
_____
_____
_____

_____

_____

_____

_____

_____

_____

_____

_____

_____

_____

_____

_____

_____

_____

_____

_____

_____

_____

_____

_____

_____

_____

_____

_____

F is for Feedback

It's also for Fear, as in fear of getting scary feedback.
Our egos are fragile and we long to hear praise,
but fear we will hear the opposite, and it makes us hesitate,
it makes us edit.
Don't.
Keep writing no matter what you hear from others,
no matter who they are.
Often I have been surprised because what I had written had
the opposite reaction to what I had feared or expected.
Either way, bad or good, I never regret having risked it.
That would be the true tragedy.

You are in charge.
Take all feedback in stride.
Wear both a thick skin and a thin skin.
It is up to you to decide if any feedback is valuable or not.
It's up to you whether you listen or not.
Sometimes, worse than receiving negative feedback,
is getting no feedback at all.
Either way, don't stop.

AUTHOR QUOTE
F is for Faulkner, William
"The artist doesn't have time to listen to the critics. The ones
who want to be writers read the reviews, the ones who
want to write don't have the time to read reviews."

_____

_____

_____

_____

_____

_____

_____

_____

_____

_____

_____

_____

_____

_____

_____

_____

_____

_____

_____

_____

_____

_____

_____

_____

_____

_____

_____

_____

_____

_____

_____

_____

_____

_____

_____

_____

_____

_____

Date: _____

Writing Project: _____

Q: What are my Fears around Feedback of this project
and how can I let them go?

_____
_____
_____
_____
_____
_____
_____
_____
_____
_____
_____
_____
_____
_____
_____
_____
_____
_____
_____
_____

_____

_____

_____

_____

_____

_____

_____

_____

_____

_____

_____

_____

_____

_____

_____

_____

_____

_____

_____

_____

_____

_____

_____

G is for Gimmick

"You gotta have a gimmick"
The title and lyrics of the famous song from the musical
Gypsy about the famous strip tease burlesque artist,
Gypsy Rose Lee, have more comfort and truth in them than
any of us want to admit.

Generally we think of gimmicks as cheap, but sometimes they
are an effective organizing principle.
Take this book, for example, I am shamelessly using the
building blocks for all words, the alphabet, as my gimmick.
Has it been done before? Hell yes, but it works.
Elizabeth Gilbert's break through book, *Eat, Pray, Love* also
had a gimmick, a structure, a context, an organizing principle.

She traveled to three countries that all start with the letter "I"
The point is, a gimmick can be a great blessing, so don't
poo-poo a gimmick, embrace it and see where it takes you.

AUTHOR QUOTE
G is for **Gilbert**, Elizabeth

"I have decided to structure it like *japa mala*, dividing my
story into 108 tales, or beads. This string of 108 tales is
further divided into three sections about Italy, India and
Indonesia – the three countries I visited during this year of
self inquiry. This division appeals to me on a personal level
because I am writing all this during my thirty-sixth year."
[36 X 3 = 108]

_____

_____

_____

_____

_____

_____

_____

_____

_____

_____

_____

_____

_____

_____

_____

_____

_____

_____

_____

_____

_____

_____

_____

_____

_____

_____

Date: _____

Writing Project: _____

Q: What's your Gimmick? If you don't have one, how might one help be an organizing principle for the project?

_____
_____
_____
_____
_____
_____
_____
_____
_____
_____
_____
_____
_____
_____
_____
_____
_____
_____
_____
_____

_____

_____

_____

_____

_____

_____

_____

_____

_____

_____

_____

_____

_____

_____

_____

_____

_____

_____

_____

_____

_____

_____

_____

_____

H is for Hit

A "hit" is fast inspiration or idea that can usually be stated in
only a few words that may have some conflict,
incongruence or double meaning.
Holiday War
Just Love
Runaway Monk
Living Out Loud

A "hit" may not be a cohesive theme but it is a little kick for
your imagination to get it started on something.
Sometimes we hear something that is a hit,
but do nothing with it.
We do not dream it any further.

We need to recognize hits, toss them around and see if they do
have a life further. Are they a legitimate exploration?

Many writers have a stash of these simple hits; they write
them down and when uninspired return to them.

AUTHOR QUOTE
H is for **Holloway, Richard**

"Simplicity, clarity, singleness: These are the attributes that
give our lives power and vividness and joy as they are also the
marks of great art. They seem to be the purpose of God for his
whole creation."

_____

_____

_____

_____

_____

_____

_____

_____

_____

_____

_____

_____

_____

_____

_____

_____

_____

_____

_____

_____

_____

_____

_____

_____

Date: _____

Writing Project: _____

Q: What was your "Hit" (inspiration), for this project?
Can you get it down to two or three words maximum?
Brainstorm your Hit or write about it, or both.

_____
_____
_____
_____
_____
_____
_____
_____
_____
_____
_____
_____
_____
_____
_____
_____
_____
_____
_____
_____
_____

_____

_____

_____

_____

_____

_____

_____

_____

_____

_____

_____

_____

_____

_____

_____

_____

_____

_____

_____

_____

_____

_____

I is for Imagination

Do you like making stuff up? That's what we did as children
without thinking it odd.
As adults, being immersed in the adult world, we have
forgotten how important it is to make believe,
and use our god-given imaginations.

Even when writing non-fiction, it is important to bridge gaps
of information with creative license.
No one loves a good storyteller for their accuracy.

Use it or lose it.
Your imagination needs exercise as much as your muscles.
If you do not exercise it regularly you may be doomed to be a
literary cripple, reliant on the crutch of banal facts and
overworked clichés.

AUTHOR QUOTE
I is for Irving, Washington
"I am always at a loss at how much to
believe of my own stories."

_____

_____

_____

_____

_____

_____

_____

_____

_____

_____

_____

_____

_____

_____

_____

_____

_____

_____

_____

_____

_____

_____

_____

_____

_____

_____

_____

_____

_____

_____

_____

_____

_____

_____

_____

_____

_____

_____

_____

_____

_____

_____

_____

_____

_____

_____

_____

_____

_____

_____

_____

_____

_____

_____

_____

_____

_____

_____

_____

_____

_____

_____

_____

_____

_____

_____

_____

_____

_____

Date: _____

Writing Project: _____

Q: How can you better use your Imagination for this project? Can you find images? Create a drawing? How can you go bigger in your Imagination to enhance this project?

_____

_____

_____

_____

_____

_____

_____

_____

_____

_____

_____

_____

_____

_____

_____

_____

_____

_____

_____

_____

_____
_____
_____
_____
_____
_____
_____
_____
_____
_____
_____
_____
_____
_____
_____
_____
_____
_____
_____
_____
_____
_____
_____

J is for Journal

Journal comes from the same origins as journey.
They are both from the root word meaning "day."
Everyday is a step on your journey, and, in the words of
Mae West, "Keep a diary, and one day it'll keep you."

A journal does not need to be kept every single day but it is
an important part of a writing habit. It is also the place you
can practice your self esteem-building, which writers, who
share their vulnerabilities when they share their words, need.
That is why there is a strong tradition
for writers to keep journals.

Journals can be mundane and routine, or colorful and
experimental. They can be whatever you want them to be.
Oscar Wilde: "I never travel without my diary. One should
always have something sensational to read on the train."

If you don't yet have a journal, start one. If you do keep one,
give yourself loud praise. This is your writing practice.

AUTHOR QUOTE
J is for **Jackson**, Helen Hunt
Wednesday, January 7, 1880 journal entry:
"did not ask her why - old woman with yellow hair -
Ah she remembered it all - green fields & gardens —
on one side this street - 17 children gathered in a minute -
threw out pennies for them - scattered like ants - six boys all
on their knees bends in one center like spokes of a wheel!"

Date: _____

Writing Project: _____

Q: Do you have a Journal for just this project? What would you like to see in this Journal? How will it help you?

_____
_____
_____
_____
_____
_____
_____
_____
_____
_____
_____
_____
_____
_____
_____
_____
_____
_____
_____
_____
_____

_____

_____

_____

_____

_____

_____

_____

_____

_____

_____

_____

_____

_____

_____

_____

_____

_____

_____

_____

_____

_____

_____

_____

K is for Knowledge

Writers are readers that are thirsty
for knowledge and stories.
They drink with gusto, but a curious thing happens.

The new knowledge percolates inside them.
Until, unbidden, they look for a way to serve it up.
With sweetener and cream,
or just straight black.

Accumulate your knowledge, escape to it,
read, and read some more.
Let it mull, let it gel, until it bubbles out.
First in notes and then in full sentences.
Serve it to us in paragraphs, or in the way that only you can.

An ample amount of knowledge is beyond dangerous.
It's sublime.

AUTHOR QUOTE
K is for **Kingsolver, Barbara**
"I'm of a fearsome mind to throw my arms around every living
librarian who crosses my path, on behalf of the souls they
never knew they saved."

_____

_____

_____

_____

_____

_____

_____

_____

_____

_____

_____

_____

_____

_____

_____

_____

_____

_____

_____

_____

_____

_____

_____

_____

_____

_____

_____

_____

_____

_____

_____

Date: _____

Writing Project: _____

Q: What Knowledge are you drawing on for this project?
What other Knowledge do you want? How are you going
to get it?

_____
_____
_____
_____
_____
_____
_____
_____
_____
_____
_____
_____
_____
_____
_____
_____
_____
_____
_____
_____

_____

_____

_____

_____

_____

_____

_____

_____

_____

_____

_____

_____

_____

_____

_____

_____

_____

_____

_____

_____

_____

_____

_____

_____

_____

_____

_____

_____

_____

L is for Laughter

Writers should want to laugh
and make others laugh too,
even the serious writers,
even ones just like you.

Laughter lifts us.
It massages, our mind, body and soul.
Art, perfectionism and lofty ideals
need not be the goal.

In laughter, we can see it!
A simpler truth:
There is no one higher, no one lower
that we cannot spoof.

Laughter makes us equals,
all ready for joy.
Be you big, be you small,
be you girl, be you boy.

So, seek laughter and play
and give it, whenever you can.
Laughter can heal,
and make all understand.

Inspired by Dr. Seuss

AUTHOR QUOTE
L is for Lake, Kathrin

"A writer has to be their own biggest fan... and they have to be able
to laugh at themselves."

_____

_____

_____

_____

_____

_____

_____

_____

_____

_____

_____

_____

_____

_____

_____

_____

_____

_____

_____

_____

_____

_____

Date: _____

Writing Project: _____

Q: How can Laughter be a part of this project? What will
it add, and where could it be added?

_____
_____
_____
_____
_____
_____
_____
_____
_____
_____
_____
_____
_____
_____
_____
_____
_____
_____
_____

_____

_____

_____

_____

_____

_____

_____

_____

_____

_____

_____

_____

_____

_____

_____

_____

_____

_____

_____

_____

_____

_____

_____

_____

_____

_____

_____

_____

M is for Muse

The concept of a Muse is an old one.
The idea that our best work comes from somewhere ethereal,
somewhere beyond ourselves, is not to be disputed
scientifically, but even if it was,
there are greater reasons to believe.

When we get our egos out of the way,
when we have silenced the voices of others,
and then turn ourselves over to whatever is there,
that is when we speak the clearest,
when both Truth and Beauty can rise to the surface.
Listen to what your Muse is telling you to write.

Allow your spark to be a spark of the world.

AUTHOR QUOTE
M is for **Morrison**, Toni
"If you surrendered to the air, you could ride it."

_____

_____

_____

_____

_____

_____

_____

_____

_____

_____

_____

_____

_____

_____

_____

_____

_____

_____

_____

_____

_____

_____

_____

Date: _____

Writing Project: _____

Q: How can you seduce your Muse? How can you listen
to her or him? Where does your Muse like to visit you?
And, under what circumstances?

_____
_____
_____
_____
_____
_____
_____
_____
_____
_____
_____
_____
_____
_____
_____
_____
_____
_____

_____

_____

_____

_____

_____

_____

_____

_____

_____

_____

_____

_____

_____

_____

_____

_____

_____

_____

_____

_____

_____

_____

_____

N is for Next!

Are you stuck in something that doesn't excite you?
What's next?
Are you almost finished a piece of writing but don't know
what you will do after it's done?
What's next?
Did you have a successful blog post with many comments but
don't know how to follow it?
What's next?
Are you writing a story that is bumbling along and you don't
know...what's next?
Remember your readers should be asking the same question.
What's going to happen next?

How can I keep my readers in suspense so they will want to
know what happens next?
Do I want to keep them hungry for what I am writing next?
Part of what separates writers from dabblers is the thinking
and planning for what is next? You are not finished when you
write one book, one essay or one poem.
This is a life long love affair.
What do you need to shake up next?

AUTHOR QUOTE

N is for **Nin**, Anais

"It is the function of art to renew our perception. What we are
familiar with we cease to see. The writer shakes up the
familiar scene, and, as if by magic, we see a new meaning in it."

_____
_____
_____
_____
_____
_____
_____
_____
_____
_____
_____
_____
_____
_____
_____
_____
_____
_____
_____
_____
_____
_____
_____
_____
_____
_____

_____

Date: _____

Writing Project: _____

Q: What happens Next? What's exciting about what happens Next?

_____
_____
_____
_____
_____
_____
_____
_____
_____
_____
_____
_____
_____
_____
_____
_____
_____
_____
_____
_____
_____
_____
_____

_____

_____

_____

_____

_____

_____

_____

_____

_____

_____

_____

_____

_____

_____

_____

_____

_____

_____

_____

_____

_____

_____

_____

O is for Opportunity to Share

Never pass up an opportunity to share our writing.
It is through sharing our words and ideas that we become
comfortable with them. We also learn and grow.

Your purpose in writing is to share. You only get better at
both writing and sharing by repeating them again and again.

Opportunities to share can be created or can be offered.
If they are offered, always say yes, ready or not.
If that unnerves you, then create opportunities to share where
you can choose the time, place and conditions.

Say yes to these opportunities, and give yourself huge praise
and pats on the back for them. You are growing in a way that
only sharing can give.
(Trepidation at sharing? See F).

AUTHOR QUOTE
O is for O'Casey, Sean
"All the world's a stage and most of us are
desperately unrehearsed."

_____

_____

_____

_____

_____

_____

_____

_____

_____

_____

_____

_____

_____

_____

_____

_____

_____

_____

_____

_____

_____

_____

_____

_____

_____

_____

_____

_____

_____

_____

_____

_____

Date: _____

Writing Project: _____

Q: Where can you find or create an Opportunity to share this work? What must happen in order to make this Opportunity possible? What one small thing do you want to get out of this Opportunity?

_____
_____
_____
_____
_____
_____
_____
_____
_____
_____
_____
_____
_____
_____
_____
_____
_____
_____

_____

_____

_____

_____

_____

_____

_____

_____

_____

_____

_____

_____

_____

_____

_____

_____

_____

_____

_____

_____

_____

_____

_____

_____

_____

_____

P is for Permission

Who gives you permission to write?
You know the answer.
It is you.
It is you every day.
It doesn't matter if you are published, unpublished,
celebrated with a wide audience,
or in a closet, shy and sharing with only a few,
or not sharing with anyone at all.

Permission to write comes from you.
Not me, not an audience, not a parent, not a teacher,
not a mentor, not an authority, not a school,
and not from any other person.
Permission to write comes from you.
It costs you nothing but time.
If you believe you want to write.
Say yes to it.

AUTHOR QUOTE

P is for Poe, Edgar Allan

"Convinced myself, I seek not to convince."

_____

_____

_____

_____

_____

_____

_____

_____

_____

_____

_____

_____

_____

_____

_____

_____

_____

_____

_____

_____

_____

_____

_____

_____

_____

Date: _____

Writing Project: _____

Q: How can you give yourself greater Permission to
write what you want to write for this project? If you had
greater Permission, how would your writing change?

_____
_____
_____
_____
_____
_____
_____
_____
_____
_____
_____
_____
_____
_____
_____
_____
_____
_____
_____
_____

_____
_____
_____
_____
_____
_____
_____
_____
_____
_____
_____
_____
_____
_____
_____
_____
_____
_____
_____
_____

_____

Q is for Questions

Never underestimate the power of a good question.
Like a great interviewer, you discover things by
being the first to ask.

Behind every piece of writing
should be a plethora of questions.
Perhaps they are questions you are trying to answer,
or think you have the answers to already.
Usually there is one essential question
behind everything you write.
Sometimes you know it,
Sometimes you don't.

Take a moment to write out the questions that you are trying
to answer. Just posing the questions can give us the clarity
that we seek.

AUTHOR QUOTE
Q is for **Quindlen,** Anna.

"All of life like a series of tableaux, and in the living we
missed so much, hid so much, left so much undone and
unsaid." …"Speech is the voice of the heart."

_____
_____
_____
_____
_____
_____
_____
_____
_____
_____
_____
_____
_____
_____
_____
_____
_____
_____
_____
_____
_____
_____
_____
_____

_____

Date: _____

Writing Project: _____

Q: What are excellent Questions to ask for this project?
Brainstorm a bunch of them without trying to answer
them.

_____

_____

_____

_____

_____

_____

_____

_____

_____

_____

_____

_____

_____

_____

_____

_____

_____

_____

_____

_____

_____

_____

_____

_____

_____

_____

_____

_____

_____

_____

_____

_____

_____

_____

_____

_____

_____

_____

_____

_____

_____

_____

_____

_____

_____

_____

_____

_____

_____

_____

_____

R is for Resistance

Resistance is the stage right before full blown procrastination.
Every writer must push through resistance and start writing.
That is why, while we write, we have to *just* write,
and not care if it is good, or who will read it,
or if it will be liked.
You can think of that another time.
A time when your writing is done.

It is important to recognize that when resistance
rears its ugly head, you will often have to
push through it and get the ball rolling
before you can get anywhere at all.

Write with your resistance,
and it will melt away.

AUTHOR QUOTE
R is for Rowling, J. K.
"If you're holding out for universal popularity, I'm afraid you
will be in this cabin for a very long time."

Joanna Kathleen Rowling,
who shortened her name to initials after being told no one would
want to read a boy's adventure written by a woman.

_____

_____

_____

_____

_____

_____

_____

_____

_____

_____

_____

_____

_____

_____

_____

_____

_____

_____

_____

_____

_____

_____

_____

_____

_____

_____

_____

Date: _____

Writing Project: _____

Q: What will be some of your habits and strategies you will use to thwart any perpetual Resistance you have to write?

_____

_____

_____

_____

_____

_____

_____

_____

_____

_____

_____

_____

_____

_____

_____

_____

_____

_____

_____

_____

_____

_____

_____

_____

_____

_____

_____

_____

_____

_____

_____

_____

_____

_____

_____

_____

_____

_____

_____

_____

_____

_____

_____

_____

S is for Story

Stories have been around much longer than written words.
They are the way we make sense of our lives,
from small adventures to great sagas.
But when you tell a story, tell us a good story,
beyond the ordinary.
A story that forces us to follow you through to the end to
find out what happened!
Tragedy.
Triumph.
Redemption.
Happiness.
How did our hero get out of trouble?
What did we learn?
Who ended up with whom?

Keeping suspense at every turn is your art.
You are a storyteller.
Carrying on one of the oldest traditions,
and *the* greatest form of communication known.
Go all out.

AUTHOR QUOTE

S is for Shakespeare, William.

"Your tale, sir, would cure deafness."

from *The Tempest*

_____

_____

_____

_____

_____

_____

_____

_____

_____

_____

_____

_____

_____

_____

_____

_____

_____

_____

_____

_____

_____

_____

_____

_____

_____

Date: _____

Writing Project: _____

Q: For this writing project, how can you create greater
suspense in telling the Story? How can you make this a
story where people have to follow it to the end?

_____

_____

_____

_____

_____

_____

_____

_____

_____

_____

_____

_____

_____

_____

_____

_____

_____

_____

_____

_____

_____

_____

_____

_____

_____

_____

_____

_____

_____

_____

_____

_____

_____

_____

_____

_____

_____

_____

_____

_____

_____

_____

_____

_____

_____

_____

_____

_____

_____

_____

_____

_____

_____

_____

_____

_____

_____

_____

T is for Time

The number one excuse for not doing your writing is
"I don't have time."
Is that true? Or is it that you have not made time?
Do you have a writing habit?
Does everything else become a priority?

If you don't make time, you are telling yourself
that writing isn't that important, and it is.

It is important not only for the results,
but the mere process of taking time to write.
Writing expands our inner selves.
When we write it is like taking our spirit to the spa,
but it doesn't cost you anything... but Time.

AUTHOR QUOTE
T is for Taylor, Susan L.
"We don't have an eternity to realize our dreams, only the
time we are here."

_____

_____

_____

_____

_____

_____

_____

_____

_____

_____

_____

_____

_____

_____

_____

_____

_____

_____

_____

_____

_____

_____

_____

_____

_____

_____

_____

_____

_____

Date: _____

Writing Project: _____

Q: What are all your ways to find Time for your writing? Consider where you will make time, both in chunks and in small snatches.

_____
_____
_____
_____
_____
_____
_____
_____
_____
_____
_____
_____
_____
_____
_____
_____
_____
_____
_____
_____
_____
_____

_____

_____

_____

_____

_____

_____

_____

_____

_____

_____

_____

_____

_____

_____

_____

_____

_____

_____

_____

_____

_____

_____

_____

_____

_____

_____

_____

_____

_____

_____

_____

_____

_____

_____

U is for Universal Truth

As writers, we are seeking a big goal, greater than gold.
The Universal, capital-T Truths.
We use the petty facts and explanations of small truths, but
will use every device at our ready to get to the real Truths
that enlighten our Universal human condition.
We will use:
Metaphors,
Similes,
Stories,
Conflict,
Comparison,
Poetry,
Provocation,
Humour,
Satire,
Pathos,
And anything that we can, to reach for that elusive Truth. We
are doomed to fail often, but keep digging nonetheless.
But when unearthed, the reader can sigh and feel her location
in the world.

AUTHOR QUOTE
U is for **Updike, John**

"Truth should not be forced; it should simply manifest itself,
like a woman who has in her privacy reflected and coolly
decided to bestow herself upon a certain man."

Date: _____

Writing Project: _____

Q: Is it time to consider what your writing is trying to
reveal? What might the Universal Truth behind it be?

_____

_____

_____

_____

_____

_____

_____

_____

_____

_____

_____

_____

_____

_____

_____

_____

_____

_____

_____

_____

_____

_____

_____

_____

_____

_____

_____

_____

_____

_____

_____

_____

_____

_____

_____

_____

_____

_____

_____

_____

_____

_____

_____

_____

_____

_____

_____

_____

V is for Vocabulary

It is only through words, their careful selection and
juxtaposition, that we create meaning. Expanding your
vocabulary is the ability to create notes for the musical score
that is your writing.
Vocabulary choices can evoke feelings.
They can be
haughty,
base,
flowery,
indulgent,
cruel,
kind,
liberating,
innocent,
noble,
or any tone you wish to create.
Play with your vocabulary, and keep a thesaurus at the ready.

AUTHOR QUOTE
V is for **Vandermeer**, Jeff

"I have always tended toward a lush prose style, but I take
care to modulate it from story to story and to strip it down
entirely when necessary."

Date: _____

Writing Project: _____

Q: How can you expand your Vocabulary for this project? What words can you use that you are not letting yourself use now?

_____
_____
_____
_____
_____
_____
_____
_____
_____
_____
_____
_____
_____
_____
_____
_____
_____
_____
_____
_____
_____

W is for Work of Words

Sometimes wordsmiths need to be banging it out
on an anvil of internal toil,
sweating through the process,
ringing out the words,
forging something hard but enduring.

Yet equal to our wordsmithing is our wordplay.
To play with words is to amuse ourselves and others.
When you combine work and play,
the work of writing
becomes a joy.

Recognize that there is a balance in your writing
of slog and dance.
This is the Work of Words.

AUTHOR QUOTE
W is for **Wilde**, Oscar
"I was working on the proof of
one of my poems all the morning,
and took out a comma.
In the afternoon I put it back again."

_____

_____

_____

_____

_____

_____

_____

_____

_____

_____

_____

_____

_____

_____

_____

_____

_____

_____

_____

_____

_____

_____

_____

_____

_____

Date: _____

Writing Project: _____

Q: For this project, what in your writing Work is slog for you? For this project, what in your writing Work is play? How can you commit to both to create your best Work?

_____
_____
_____
_____
_____
_____
_____
_____
_____
_____
_____
_____
_____
_____
_____
_____
_____
_____
_____
_____

X is for X-tra!

EXTRA! EXTRA!
Read all about it!
How can you give more in your writing?
How can you give eXtra, for an eXtraordinary eXperience?

Extra rarely means more words.
X
It means thinking beyond your usual responses.
X
It means sharing what no one else has dared to share.
X
It means deeper background work.
X
It means coming up with the defining question.
X
It means bringing in another voice, another opinion.
X
It means taking more risks to share the words you believe in.
X
How can you take it to the next level by providing
X-tra!

AUTHOR QUOTE

X is for X, Malcolm
"Anytime you see someone more successful than you are,
they are doing something you aren't."

_____

_____

_____

_____

_____

_____

_____

_____

_____

_____

_____

_____

_____

_____

_____

_____

_____

_____

_____

_____

_____

_____

_____

_____

_____

_____

_____

_____

_____

_____

_____

_____

_____

_____

Date: _____

Writing Project: _____

Q: How can you add X-tra to this writing project? (See X)

_____
_____
_____
_____
_____
_____
_____
_____
_____
_____
_____
_____
_____
_____
_____
_____
_____
_____
_____
_____
_____
_____
_____

Y is for You

Are you forgetting something?
Are you forgetting **You** in your writing?
Sometimes we try to hide behind words, when this
is the time to reveal who we really are.

You are unique, and when people read your writing they want
to know you,
your thoughts,
your passions,
your feelings,
your lessons,
your triumphs,
your tragedies,
your stories,
your wisdom,
your stupidity,
your vulnerabilities,
your strength.

This is where the soul of connection to your reader happens.
What part of you have you not included?
How can you put **You** into your writing?

AUTHOR QUOTE
Y is for **Young, Marguerite**
"All creatures are flawed, but out of the flaw
may come the universe."

_____

_____

_____

_____

_____

_____

_____

_____

_____

_____

_____

_____

_____

_____

_____

_____

_____

_____

_____

_____

_____

_____

_____

_____

_____

_____

_____

_____

_____

Date: _____

Writing Project: _____

Q: How can you better add You to this writing project?
How could it be beneficial?

_____
_____
_____
_____
_____
_____
_____
_____
_____
_____
_____
_____
_____
_____
_____
_____
_____
_____
_____
_____
_____
_____

_____

_____

_____

_____

_____

_____

_____

_____

_____

_____

_____

_____

_____

_____

_____

_____

_____

_____

_____

_____

_____

_____

_____

_____

_____

_____

_____

_____

_____

Z is for Zen

Breathe and let a word come to you.
Or just breathe.
Wait.
Be patient.
Or be impatient.
But wait.
Stare up in the sky.
Watch clouds drift by.
Sit at a café.
Watch people drift by.
Watch. Listen. Wait.
No one will need to tell you when to write.
You will already be writing.

AUTHOR QUOTES
Z is for **Zola and Zelazny**

"I am an artist... I am here to live out loud."
Emile Zola

"I try to sit down at the typewriter four times a day, even if
it's only five minutes, and write three sentences."
Roger Zelazny

_____

_____

_____

_____

_____

_____

_____

_____

_____

_____

_____

_____

_____

_____

_____

_____

_____

_____

_____

_____

_____

_____

_____

_____

_____

Date: _____

Writing Project: _____

Q: Give yourself some Zen writing time. Pen. Paper. Breath. How long can you wait before something comes to you that you want to write down? Find out.

_____
_____
_____
_____
_____
_____
_____
_____
_____
_____
_____
_____
_____
_____
_____
_____
_____
_____
_____
_____

_____

_____

_____

_____

_____

_____

_____

_____

_____

_____

_____

_____

_____

_____

_____

_____

_____

_____

_____

_____

_____

_____

_____

_____

_____

_____

_____

_____

_____

_____

_____

_____

_____

_____

_____

_____

_____

About the Author

When Kathrin Lake was eight, she made up stories, cast the other kids in parts, raided her mother's closet and then started rehearsals immediately. Much later she studied theatre and film at Simon Fraser University in Vancouver, B.C. Although she developed a passion for non-fiction by writing for the campus paper and later other external publications, it was being in the Theatre that reignited her storytelling days as a child. She collaborated with award-winning Canadian playwrights Marc Diamond and Guillermo Verdecchia and even formed a brief writing partnership with the late, great, comedy writer, Irwin Barker, who would go on to write for Rick Mercer (in Canada he is the equivalent of David Letterman). She has won awards and prizes in playwriting, but on a dare, started a community newspaper in the happening Vancouver arts neighbourhood called *The Drive*. She has taught writing for over 20 years and has authored other books, such as *From Survival to Thrival* and *Writing with Cold Feet*.

Kathrin is currently a full time writer, educator, professional speaker and founder of the *Vancouver School of Writing*. Through the school, she teaches and has a writing retreat in Mexico for new authors in all genres.

kathrinlake.com   vancouverschoolofwriting.com

CPSIA information can be obtained
at www.ICGtesting.com
Printed in the USA
LVHW020432010523
745722LV00014B/1216